USING THIS BOOK

*Children learn to read by **reading**, but they need help to begin with.*

When you have read the story on the left-hand pages aloud to the child, go back to the beginning of the book and look at the pictures together.

Encourage children to read the sentences under the pictures. If they don't know a word, give them a chance to 'guess' what it is from the illustrations, before telling them.

There are more suggestions for helping children to learn to read in the *Parent/Teacher* booklet.

British Library Cataloguing in Publication Data

McCullagh, Sheila K.
  Danger in the Magician's garden. — (Puddle Lane series).
  I. Title   II. Morris, Tony   III. Series
  428.6   PR6063.A165/

  ISBN 0-7214-1071-5

First edition

Published by Ladybird Books Ltd Loughborough Leicestershire UK
Ladybird Books Inc Lewiston Maine 04240 USA

© Text and layout SHEILA McCULLAGH MCMLXXXVIII
© In publication LADYBIRD BOOKS LTD MCMLXXXVIII
Printed in England

Danger in the Magician's garden

written by SHEILA McCULLAGH
illustrated by TONY MORRIS

This book belongs to:

Ladybird Books

It was a fine, warm evening.
The Wideawake Mice were all out
in the Magician's garden.

Uncle Maximus and Aunt Matilda
were sitting on a tree root,
by the hollow tree,
when Jeremy came home
with a sack full of nuts.

Jeremy came home
with a sack full of nuts.

"Where did you find these?"
asked Uncle Maximus,
helping himself to a nut.
"On the steps of the Magician's house,"
said Jeremy. "There are lots more.
Bits of cheese, too, and cake crumbs."
"I think I'll go and see for myself,"
said Uncle Maximus.
He climbed down from the tree root.
"I'll come too," said Aunt Matilda.

"I'll just put this sack inside,
and then I'll come and
show you the way," said Jeremy.

6

Jeremy said,
"The nuts were on the steps
of the Magician's house."

Jeremy left the sack in the big hole
under the hollow tree,
and then he set off with
Uncle Maximus and Aunt Matilda
towards the Magician's house.

Jeremy left the sack
in the big hole
under the tree.

Jeremy led the way through the grass,
climbing over rocks and
running under bushes.
Before they had gone very far,
Uncle Maximus was out of breath.
"Isn't there an easier way to go?"
he panted.

"Yes, there is," said Jeremy.
"But this is the safest way."

"Safest!" cried Uncle Maximus.
"Do you mean that it's **dangerous**,
out here in the garden?"

"Well, you don't know
who might be about," said Jeremy.

Jeremy led the way.

"I'm going back," said Uncle Maximus.
"I don't feel very well."

"Don't you want any cake crumbs?"
asked Jeremy.

Uncle Maximus looked very unhappy.
"Of course I do," he said, rather crossly.
"But I can't get to the steps and back.
I'm not well. I can't do it."

"You go home, Maximus,"
said Aunt Matilda.
"I'll go on with Jeremy, and
bring some crumbs back for you."

"I – I think I **will** go home,"
said Uncle Maximus.
"I don't feel at all well."

"I'm going back,"
said Uncle Maximus.

Uncle Maximus went back
to the hollow tree,
and Jeremy went on with Aunt Matilda.
Suddenly, a blackbird in a tree
over their heads began to scold.
Aunt Matilda stopped.
"What's that blackbird saying?"
she asked.
"I don't know," said Jeremy.
He sniffed the air.
"Can you smell anything?" he asked.
"There's a very strange smell,"
said Aunt Matilda. "I don't like it."
"Nor do I," said Jeremy.

Aunt Matilda stopped.

At that moment, a big fox
jumped out from behind a bush.
He seized Aunt Matilda in his mouth.

Jeremy leapt sideways, behind some stones.
He peeped out between two of the stones,
and saw the fox standing there,
with Aunt Matilda in his jaws.

A big fox jumped out.

Jeremy was very frightened,
but he wasn't going to run away
if there was a chance
of saving Aunt Matilda.

He poked his head up over a stone.
"Put her down!" he cried.
"You mustn't hurt anyone
in the Magician's garden.
The Magician said so."

"Put her down!"
cried Jeremy.

The fox put Aunt Matilda
down on the ground, and
held her there with his paw.
He was planning to eat Aunt Matilda
for supper, but he thought that,
if only Jeremy would come a little nearer,
he might have **two** mice for supper,
not just one.
"The Magician said nothing to me,"
he said. "I don't live in his garden.
I live in the wood."

The fox put
Aunt Matilda down.
He said, ''I don't live
in the Magician's garden.''

"I don't care where you live,"
said Jeremy. "I'll tell the Magician.
When the Magician finds out
that you've hurt Aunt Matilda,
you'll be sorry!"

"I'm a little deaf," said the fox.
"I can't hear what you say.
Come nearer."

Jeremy said,
''I will tell the Magician.''

Two heads appeared over the bushes.
Hari and Gita had been playing ball
in the Magician's garden.
They were going home,
when they heard a noise, and
they stopped to see what it was.

Hari and Gita
looked over a bush.
They saw the fox.

As they looked, the fox made
a sudden leap towards Jeremy.
Hari still had the ball in his hand.
As quick as a flash,
he threw it straight at the fox.
"Get off!" he cried. "Get away!"

"Get off!" cried Hari.
"Get away!"

The ball hit the fox in mid-air.
It didn't hurt him, but it startled him.
Jeremy ducked down behind some stones.
The fox dropped to the ground.
He saw Hari and Gita, and
ran off under the bushes.
Hari and Gita chased after him.

The fox saw Hari and Gita.
He ran off, under the bushes.

Jeremy came out from behind the stones,
and ran to Aunt Matilda.
She was struggling to her feet.
Her dress was all torn and muddy,
and she could scarcely stand.
Aunt Matilda shook her head.
She couldn't speak.

Jeremy ran to Aunt Matilda.

Jeremy helped her to limp
across to the stones.
"Wait here for a bit," he said.
"You'll be quite safe here. Look —
there's a little hole under this stone.
We can hide in that."
They crept under the stone, and waited.
They could hear Hari and Gita shouting,
a long way away.

Jeremy and Aunt Matilda hid.
They could hear Hari and Gita.

The shouting stopped.
Jeremy came out of the hole.
The blackbird had stopped scolding,
and was down on the ground,
looking for worms.
Jeremy sniffed the air.
The fox had gone.

Jeremy came out of the hole.
The fox had gone.

Jeremy went back to Aunt Matilda.
"It's safe to go home now," he said.

"I don't know if I can,"
whispered poor Aunt Matilda.
"I'm almost too frightened to move."

"We must go while it's safe,"
said Jeremy. "I'll go first."

He crept out of the hole, and
Aunt Matilda limped after him.

Jeremy went back to
Aunt Matilda.
"We must go home," he said.

A few minutes later, the two little mice
crept safely back down the mousehole,
and under the hollow tree.
The other mice were all there.
They had heard Hari and Gita shouting,
and had run home as fast as they could.

"I'll never go into the garden again,"
said Uncle Maximus, when he heard
what had happened.

"Someone will have to go,"
said Aunt Jane.
"We have to go out, to find food.
But we'll be very careful."

"You have to be careful all the time,
when you're a real wood mouse,"
said Chestnut.

The Wideawake Mice
were all at home
in the hole under the tree.

Hari and Gita came back
through the garden, looking for the mice.
But the mice had gone.
"They must be all right," said Hari.
"They must have gone home."

"We must tell the Magician
about that fox," said Gita.

"Yes, we must," said Hari.
"It's not safe for the mice,
with a fox in the garden."
They went back into Puddle Lane.

Hari and Gita looked for the
mice, but the mice had gone.

"We must tell the Magician,"
said Gita.

Notes for the parent/teacher

When you have read the story, go back to the beginning. Look at each picture and talk about it, pointing to the caption below, and reading it aloud yourself.

Run your finger along under the words as you read, so that the child learns that reading goes from left to right. (You needn't say this in so many words. Children learn many useful things about reading by just reading with you, and it is often better to let them learn by experience, rather than by explanation.) When you next go through the book, encourage the child to read the words and sentences under the illustrations.

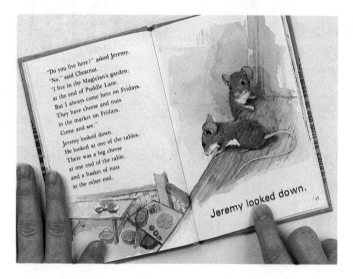

Don't rush in with the word before she* has time to think, but don't leave her struggling for too long. Always encourage her to feel that she is reading successfully, praising her when she does well, and avoiding criticism.

Now turn back to the beginning, and print the child's name in the space on the title page, using ordinary, not capital letters. Let her watch you print it: this is another useful experience.

*Children enjoy hearing the same story many times. Read this one as often as the child likes hearing it. The more opportunities she has of looking at the illustrations and **reading** the captions with you, the more she will come to recognise the words. Don't worry if she **remembers** rather than **reads** the captions. This is a normal stage in learning.*

If you have a number of books, let her choose which story she would like to have again.

There are two other stories about the fox.
The Magician comes into both the stories, but
the first one is about the Wideawake Mice, and
the second is about the two cats, Tim and Tessa
Catchamouse.

Stage 2

13 The fox and
the Magician

from
The fox and
the Magician

14 Adventure in
the wood

from
Adventure
in the wood